Losing my Misery

a collection of poems

Bobby Long

Copyright © 2016 Bobby Long
All Rights Reserved

This book is copyright in all countries.

First Edition 2016

SGO MUSIC PUBLISHING LTD
PO Box 2015 Salisbury SP2 7WU UK
www.sgomusic.com

ABOUT THE AUTHOR

Robert "Bobby" Long was born in Wigan, Lancashire, England in 1985. Son of Chris and Tania. Grandson of Tom, Edna, Douglas and Jean. A recording and touring artist who resides in New York City with his wife Nicole and two pets, Lucille and Isis. *Losing My Misery* is the follow up to his first book of poetry, *Losing My Brotherhood* (2012). His interests aside from music and writing are Christmas, drinking, Manchester United and The Wigan Warriors.

CREDITS

Illustrations by Bobby Long

Edited by Sharon Weisz and Nicole D'Anna

Cover Design by Sparetire Design
sparetiredesign.com

Cover Illustration by Hilary Huckins-Weidner
hilaryhuckinsweidner.com

Back Cover Photo by Bobby Long

Editorial Advisor: Stuart Ongley

www.bobbylong.info
tdmsongsentertainment@gmail.com

Dedicated to the memory, love and talent of Brett Robinson Kilroe

CONTENTS

	Page
Gotta Get Out	1
Ancient Cracks	3
Cafe Table Visions	4
It's Good to Miss Someone	6
Dark Road	7
Night Bird	9
That Sweet Refrain	10
Christmas Lights	11
O'Sister	12
A Parisian	14
Awoken Clean	16
A Writer's Life	19
Love Is Sweet	21
Angela-Louise	22
Keeping Apart	24
Stare Down	25
Blue Cagoule	27
Real Love	28
The Shiny Penny	30
Blood Pumps Lilac	31
Secular For Jesus	32
First Memory	35
Martyr	37
It's Good to See a Little Brightness	38
Headless In Ohio	40
Picking a Carcass Clean	41
Quiet Hollow	42
When Loved	43
New Year's Eve	44

	Page
The Only Way Is Hope	45
Kill Someone	47
O' Sweet Marie	49
I Will Never	50
Death To The Womb	52
My Favourite Hotel Diner	55
I Wonder	56
Irish Poem	57
Sleeping with the Diamond	59
Tulum	61
The Town Green	62
On To The Next	63
WebMD and Google	64
Jealous Of Me	66
Poem 99	67
Pie in the Sky	69
De-Pre-SS-Ion	70
455	72
The Rain in the Mountain	75
Lay It Down	77
The War	78
Inner City	79
You Me, You Me	80
Let It Out, Let It Go	81
Shirley and Iver	82
South of France	85
Another Angle	91
In The Darkest of Days	92
Please Be Understanding and Kind	93

GOTTA GET OUT

My parents were born and raised
in some dead end town,
where the dole is up and your life is down,
where your kids they play out in the street,
and the water seeps into their feet

My parents were kids in some dead end town,
where you pledged allegiance to the Crown,
where the school spat you out at the age of fifteen,
and the men scrap and the women clean

My parents met in some dead end town,
at a community hall, head to toe in brown,
where they fell in love and pledged to marry,
then all they had was what they could carry

My parents they worked in some dead end town,
fifteen hour days just to survive then drown,
my dad worked as a fireman but broke his leg,
so he worked day shifts
and went to night school instead

My parents had me in some dead end town,
I was born in the same hospital in the same white gown,
and they chose to move away and stop the rot,
so they packed up their house, my bottle and cot

My parents then moved into a dead end place,
to give me everything they hadn't and change my fate,
to scrape a living away from the constant drone,
to get myself closer to the throne

I went to school in a dead end place,
with the same lack of education and the same white face,
where although I was no better, no different or worse,
my Northern accent was often a working class curse

I was raised and grew older in a dead end place,
where your hope was to get out and join a rat race,
where the finishing line was somewhere far,
from the same old stories in the same old bar

I was told to get out of this dead end place,
and bided my time to make an escape,
my parents divorced under the pressure of living,
of paying the mortgage and feeding three children

I feel like most of my friends don't see this dead end town,
It's like a deep black hole under an invisible gown,
my friends they see me being silently led,
and though some of them are earnest,
some of them are dead

So I'm writing this from the dead end city, Mam and Dad,
I'm doing my best to turn the past to history,
I'm toiling the streets and riding the aches and pain,
but I'll never live in a dead end town again

ANCIENT CRACKS

Waiting for the night to befall
And nothing matters anymore
But ancient cracks they fill.

When water turns to ice inside the cracks
and breaks the stone mould
And the heat turns the ice to air
Not a trace that it was ever there.

And I'm left to the blue wonder
wondering whatever happens
to me in the darkness
And I'm never going back
Never going back.

CAFE TABLE VISIONS

You sit down slowly, your eyes underpinned,
spinning your mind for the last time you sinned,
like a rosy red apple continuously skinned,
half the words golden, the other half binned

Open, exposed, a cleric of what's right,
standing for the left when it's time to write.

Forgotten dreams and your life undercooked,
you write the first line and quickly you're hooked,
you dream of the cover, when it will be booked,
by the fourth line you're lost and clearly your fucked

Sit back in your chair and dream of the night,
one foot in the dark whenever you write.

Writer of the free or scavenger of the rhyme,
Google the meaning half of the time,
make sure the words add up in every line,
stay close to the edge without committing a crime

Your influences are deep, but kept out of sight,
so your conscience is clean whenever you write.

Where vultures fly is where you wish to dare,
to rip up your mind and write of the tear,
and to keep the viewer present and always aware,
that your writing straight from the lion's lair

Please let the masses notice this worthy fight,
of me kneeling to the gods whenever I write.

O will I become a masterful son,
of the use of a quip, a joke or a pun,
like to say something has ended but has only begun,
o why is this rhyme so boringly fun

I'll scamper to the edge like when a bird takes flight,
to flutter the language when I begin to write.

It's the way and the path this unruly life,
where you wallow in riches and dream up your strife,
begging for protection while holding a knife,
your enemy is wallowing and self decay is rife

You walk up the ladder to the highest of heights,
and are bound to fall whenever you write.

IT'S GOOD TO MISS SOMEONE

Bring down the Tennessee light cloud,
let the sunbeams fire through the trees,
and light up the ground.
For you, my love, I'll take away the light,
bring it back to New York,
for the long winter I'm gone.

Don't we fare the weather together,
so we can also fare the weather alone,
and I'll be home soon.
You can forget the way you feel right now,
and I'll forget too,
It's good to miss someone.

DARK ROAD

Dark road is coming,
the tyres are humming,
into Eastern Ohio with my gums a-bleeding.
Talking of nuance and conferring about sleeping,
hoping that fate and hope won't come when I'm dreaming.
Dark road is coming with blazing saddles,
but comedy left me alone in the darkness.
My friend is from Georgia, and I am from England,
And somewhere between the tyres are humming.

Oh dark road, oh dark road
go leave me alone,
find another cursed human being and find a home

Sulk off into the night, leave the road alone for me,
it's the closest I feel to being free.

Night Bird

NIGHT BIRD

The call from the night bird is eerie and bright,
untraceable as nature's ghost takes flight,
I imagine my very last and dying breath,
steeped in much mystery as I come to death.

Like the night bird cast in constant shroud,
the call to end is neither quiet nor loud,
the end is walked in shadow and dark,
not like the calling of the morning lark.

We humans we prey on others around,
and force upon that mortal sound,
we bomb and spray our metal vine,
far from the honour of the old front line.

Our opinions are cast upon the screen,
on articles read but never seen,
we sentence to death those who look and seem,
a little like those in our darkest dream.

We try to stop hate by hating the breed,
and pass on to our youth that wisdom by seed.

The night bird is beautiful left alone to the dark,
seen but not heard unlike the morning lark.

THAT SWEET REFRAIN

Had I not lingered awhile
I would not have you
I would not have New York City
and my dog Lucille
and my cat (Isis) with the unfortunate name
I would not have anything

I may have been richer had I never met you
had I not lingered awhile
I may be more successful and have better reviews
or more people at my shows,
I may be a better writer
and better to write this poem
so you could understand its meaning better
and feel what I'm trying to say

But I would not have you
but for that sweet refrain I took against the tidal grain
I would not have anything.

CHRISTMAS LIGHTS

If I had to be something
hanging from your Christmas tree,
I would not be the brightest one,
or the clearest one to see.

I would not be the ribboned swinger,
that turns in winter's draft,
I would not be the bright shiner,
or one made with loving craft.

I would not be the teased ribbons,
or the chocolates wrapped in foil,
I couldn't stand to be the tinsel,
I would feel guilty of the toil.
I'm too bashful to be an angel
sat proudly at the head,
or a religious bauble staring back
filling you with dread.

I would like to be your Christmas lights,
brightening the dim,
waiting for you to get home from work
so you can plug me in.

O'SISTER

So tie the snarling dog to the bench post,
and leave the bike wheel turning round,
those who hurt you once were right to,
but only in the coward's logic was it found

leave the baby to me for the evening,
he will not seek to feel your love,
for I am too your father's child,
and we both carry the same blood

and as the baby grows to be a little older,
do not take his tongue for truth,
for now he is his father's son,
when he bites down with his front tooth

for he is a lamb to the slaughter,
and halfway bred to cause you pain,
for he mirrors what he sees,
and you will see that man's face again

but as he reaches an age of reason,
of educated and reasoned love,
no son can turn against his mother,
for he also sees his own tortured blood

and as the child turns to man,
his own father will turn away,
for he cannot melt and bend a boy,
who stands firmly in his way

and you o dearest mother,
and you our dearest friend,
release the snarling dog you once tied,
and nature makes amends

the father crawls into the pits of lonely,
but never retraces what he's done,
once bred from the devil,
now living in his slum.

A PARISIAN

I long to be a Parisian.
To smoke cigarettes in the honeycomb of the catacombs
and to write long words upon the Seine.
I long to pretend I'm not turned by the Eiffel Tower
and to ride a peddled moped.
I will not wonder about the marks
on the sides of historic buildings,
and who kissed and leaned upon them.
I will not linger, I promise.
But I realize I will always just be a joyous visitor,
a part time plastic Parisian,
linked only through the spirit
and the longing of some indifferent dream.

I want to sit presently in the smoke and ash
of the cafe near Sacre Coeur,
though never go in and check the graves,
but I promise to snivel at those who do.
Then I would be on my way
to visit a grandmother with pastries, as I bustle with
purpose through the small intertwining streets
and walk past ex-girlfriends who broke my heart,
their perfume laced onto my shoulder forever.
I will have woe etched into my heart
that Parisian girls are too beautiful to tame,
as I tell a tourist near my wicker chair
in my favourite cafe, where they know my name.
I will long to be finished with Paris, and never return,
leaving a room for another soul
to feed and ramble honestly up the steps.
Because it will always be a part of me,
scarred from my own romantic vision.

Scarred from the journey I chose to undertake,
some years ago,
long before now.

AWOKEN CLEAN

Today let the bright light shine,
fill my room with echoes from the outside,
street crawlers and noisemakers crowd under my window,
for today I have awoken clean.

Let the earth spin slower,
somehow let the light not dim,
friends they call with their fickle tomfoolery,
make plans for me to keep,
for today I have awoken clean.

Note me present for your future endeavours,
let the ebb and flow carry me without a word of negativity,
bring out your longest recipes for dinner,
for today I have awoken clean

Play me your newest love on the radio,
and I'll find peace in its reverbed hi-frequency snare drum,
not forgetting to forget any circumstantial comparatives,
for today I have awoken clean.

Let's walk the street and find eye contact,
let's supper with strangers
and buy drinks for beautiful women,
stay out till the birds both rest and sing,
for today I have awoken clean.

Flutter our weekly spending on lottery and whim,
build a bridge only to tear it down,
walk over the ground like we have been here before,
for today I have awoken clean.

Lay to rest my day and leave any struggle
with clothes lifeless on the floor
spared to feel anything at all,
just like me as I fall softly to sleep,
for today I had awoken unclean.

A Writer's Life

A WRITER'S LIFE

My face is unwashed,
my sink is full,
my back is sore from shoveling snow,
another day in God's paradise,
yet I'm craving for more and seeking his will.

I want a place without command or order,
a place with string that dangles from the sky,
so I can tie my things,
then pull the strings,
and let my demons die.

I only know a few things well,
and the rest I pretend to see and reap.
I walk the parks and watch the trees,
what I hate I send, what I love I keep.

Last year was the year,
and the year before and before,
last year was Eden, this year hell,
both only imagination
that only time can tell.

Life is long to those who love,
and short to those who don't,
aging is comfort for those with pain,
aging is deadly for those without pain,
and fame, you never choose the fame.

I only know a few things well,
and the rest I pretend to see and reap.

I walk the parks and watch the trees,
what I hate I send, what I love I keep.

My hands are soft,
some say my work isn't work at all,
but my back is sore from shoveling snow,
another day in God's paradise, to test the grace,
but it will be tomorrow when I see his face.

So listen when you speak,
the endless songs fill up my book,
I wrote them myself with these soft hands,
what is mine is mine, what is theirs I took.

LOVE IS SWEET

Real love is hard to find
but I think I got it
you are not meant to know
but I'm finding myself caught up in something that's sweet
sweet enough to cover the bland
and entice me when I'm full
one last taste before I truly fill up
to help the medicine go down
to reward myself when I've done good
and to hurt when I have done wrong
like a bad diet pill
and the un-natural weight I've lost is you
it hurts like stolen Halloween candy
you've seen those kids crying
ready to let themselves
be swallowed up and adopted
it's pretty sweet
but it doesn't come once a year
it's hard to find.

ANGELA-LOUISE

I had a dirty afternoon with Angela-Louise
who wore socks up to her knees
behind the school beyond the trees
she was a crook with forty thieves
who unclipped my belt, rolled up her sleeves
there was no stopping Angela-Louise

She bit my neck and made me wince
she was my queen, I was her prince
she kissed my lips and made me flinch,
where many had been, not been back since,
my glasses carried her fingerprints,
like a vampire's need to kill and tease,
I was up to my neck with Angela-Louise

I tried to run but she made me stay,
and wouldn't let romance get in the way,
her friend was a lookout and hid in the grey,
I spotted her looking but I dared not say,
Angela-Louise took my pain away,
and suddenly I felt like the summer breeze,
made into a man by Angela Louise

I did not know what to give in return.
for she gave me enough, and I had much to learn,
left with a strand of her hair the colour auburn,
I had lost my heart to the deepest cavern,
somewhere between East Germany and a wild Western,
she had sung my song from the highest lectern,
I had walked in fresh, and now I'm post-modern,
born in the north but talking southern,

lost to a place in the pit of Hades,
I'm deep in the depths with Angela-Louise

It had been a few days, I was walking on home,
she had told me to sit and wait by the phone,
I saw her there talking to my best friend Jerome,
my heart died and sank as she threw him a bone,
her friend saw me watching and called out in drone,
I was caught on the peak sleeping in the death zone,
I ran through the woods like a tempestuous cyclone,
tears from my eyes and a pre-written tombstone,
foul to the game on the skin of my knees
I'd been had by a girl named Angela-Louise

KEEPING APART

She woke up this morning, ten to nine
laying there still, the covers fenced her like brine
but the troubled don't trouble with time,
when the most downhill part feels like an ice climb,

        sat there in the dark,
        keeping apart.

He waited in the other room, still,
and the clocks tick-tock, constant, the echoed shrill,
the blood rushed to his face and the pills,
jingle jangled their way from his eyes to the sill,

        sat there in the dark,
        keeping apart.

She entered into the room, blind, pale
the lamp burst into light, proving darkness frail,
he points to the window sill,
she digests and kneels, bowing to the drug frill,

        sat there in the dark,
        keeping apart.

He echoes her heart, her beats, and drone,
wintered life outside,
feels more like warmth and home,
the train tracks usher the rickety tone,
of her in her nightgown, with child, all alone,

        sat there in the dark,
        keeping apart

STARE DOWN

Sometimes you are awoken from the reality
that sits deep inside
you find the mundane beauty of life,
paper on the wind, stars, endless stars
something trivial,
and you finally look around,
scared, amused, confused
just two eyes inside a round head,
and you have a second to ask questions,
of your very existence
and why you of all came to be.
For inside those ticking lessons,
you finally get to see,
the need for ignorance,
for that light can blind and leave a man insane,
like so many who walk
the whitewashed walls of an asylum,
and they cannot awake from the spell,
it is good to not stare too long,
into the colours of insanity,
and into the tones of reality.

Blue Cagoule

BLUE CAGOULE

I went to school in my blue cagoule,
drenched to the hip like a swimming pool,
like I'd been wading marshes on a milking stool,
my teeth they needed dental school,
when I went to school in my blue cagoule.

She stood there looking all dry and pretty,
her Mum had driven her, she worked in the city,
the teacher took off my shorts in front of a committee,
ha ha ha, you can see his thingy,
I said the winter rain was awful nippy,
standing there dazed like a Woodstock hippie,
I went to school in my blue cagoule,
playing the lover, treated the fool.

I played the recorder, she played the violin,
she smelled of flowers, I dreamt of the sin,
her hands too delicate to line any bin,
she's all too familiar with Arabian satin,
my blue cagoule rolled up in my plastic bag,
her coat hung on the pegs looked like a proud white stag.

A few years later, I smelled the grass,
I was below her line, she was upper class,
I was all too familiar, a maundering black mass,
I ate frozen fish fingers, she ate sea bass,
I drank from the bottle, she drank from the glass,
I should have known that day back in school,
she would never like me in my wet blue cagoule.

REAL LOVE

I loved you so much back then,
so much so that I could not talk to you,
though under playground rule we were wed.

I would run home from school
and dream of you in the night,
I would run around the fields and dream of you.
With jumpers for goal posts,
I would score goals in your name.
Falling asleep listening to the Beatles
I would sing "Real Love" to you in assembly
in front of the mothers in my youthful dreams.

I loved you so much I played cello to your clarinet,
I loved you so much I ran away from you.
When we studied a royal namesake in class,
my heart jumped, and I became angry and jealous.
Then one day I kissed someone
who looked like a Spice Girl,
"Just like little girls and boys," Lennon said.
I sold myself that day, lost to a media machine,
and my real love was undone.

I tried to take it back
but a traitor had already told you and your friends,
so on your birthday you cried because of me.
I walked home sobbing while eating
the chocolate birthday present I had picked for you.
I never played cello again,
and I was forever just a simple boy to the other girls,
no longer a romantic simpleton
directed by his heart.

Forever more a driven shark,
a seeker of reputation and flesh.
So long, wherever you may be.
I still hear your name and think of you.

THE SHINY PENNY

The last moon of winter
the shiny penny
struck out on Cold and Ice
swinging for our fences.
Forced to leave with Father Time,
we will go outside tomorrow
and seek spring.
Our four-faced moon,
been with us for awhile
will be with us forever,
long after we're gone,
that shiny penny,
he'll be back,
don't count on him,
not coming back too soon

BLOOD PUMPS LILAC

I lost myself
for a horrible second
under the stars

and I could not escape
the weighted pressure
of the sharp light
while my blood pumps lilac
inside my veins.

only you

you can take me back
and rid me from the sight
of myself
of my destiny
while my blood pumps lilac
inside my veins.

if you stay
and you don't have to
I don't think I'll ever be rid of this secret hell,
smeared with sadness
but the sun will shine a bit brighter today
if you stay
and tomorrow my blood will pump lilac
inside my veins
but you will have stayed
so I'll be okay.

SECULAR FOR JESUS

Those heady days of falling autumn,
your grandma came to rest,
you rebelled against your parents
and didn't wear a dress,
I said that you looked beautiful in spite of what you'd lost,
too secular for Jesus,
but you lay yourself upon the cross

You left me to a winter too cold for any coat
You're an isolated castle, and I'm drowning in your moat,
too low for any limbo, too high for any crane,
too secular for Jesus,
too strong for any wane

You left me out in summer,
and I burned under the sun,
your arms were folded softly,
your hair tied in a bun,
oh why not wake me slowly and try to call me in,
you're too secular for Jesus
and don't care about the sin

The spring was quick and steady
and you had enough of me,
you balanced your words so coldly
and you needed to be free,
oh why did you wait the year
to rid me like a curse,
and now you mention Jesus
amid your favourite Bible verse

Since those days I've moved on slowly
and no one sees hide nor hair of you,
you preach with one hand on the Hippocratic oath,
another on the pew,
you're walking slowly with your Lord,
now he's your taming of the shrew,
I'm too secular for Jesus,
I'm too secular for you.

First Memory

FIRST MEMORY

My father sang about the gallows tree,
the poor man waiting to be hung,
what a thing to sing to a small boy,
songs of a man with his neck to be rung

He sang it on a Sunday evening,
after me and my sisters had a bath,
we listened cleanly about the poor man's family,
not able to stop the hangman wrath

He stood there on the wooden deck,
and looked down on his family of three,
as they said one at a time,
"yes, I have come to see you hanging
from the gallows tree."

Just as all hope had been lost,
and the tears had filled our eyes
my father's voice, it heightened,
and his eyes hit the skies

"Slack your rope hangman,
here comes his one true love,"
a darling beauty riding on horseback,
his angel from above

My father hugged my mother,
and told us all to go to bed,
for she had saved her poor hanging love,
and he did not need to sing about the dead

Still I don't know what to make about this song,
    filled with horror, rescue and strife,
    I guess your family will abandon you,
    unlike a true love, unlike your wife.

MARTYR

Too scared to write
and tell others about the things you fear the most,
in case they come true.

As you will be given a certain title,
a commendation of survival,
despite the things you live with,
and be that guy forever.

The guy who has something,
who lives within the fearful fear
of stressful days,
but keeps his chin up
as two legs fill with the weary,
and keeps it all inside.

Bottled gases and groans,
personal planets colliding and reacting,
but withholding yourself from giving it up,
you will at least be free from other's worry,
and free from the title of a martyr,
who dies a little every day.

IT'S GOOD TO SEE A LITTLE BRIGHTNESS

I want you to stay awhile, maybe an hour or two,
let's discuss the vast and open plain
or what you deem to be the truth.
Let's cover the blanket over our heads, set the light to dim,
part the curtains, keep the torch,
to let the brightness in.

I hadn't met you that long ago, maybe a year or three,
when you picked me out of a busy room
and sat upon my knee.
We drove all night in my washed out car,
and you kissed me on my chin,
but I wouldn't stop driving until first light,
to let the brightness in.

So here we are, you and me,
I see it's you and me.
A little darkness didn't hurt no one,
but my heart hates the lies that it has spun,
under the cover of night, without the light to see,
I see it's you and me.

The scalpel blade is hinged upon the open eye that sees,
let's turn our heads to the future's cut,
and understand our sin.
Sometimes it's good for it to shine,
and test out the knowledge that we have learned,
and understand our crime.

No, we're not heading back to any time or age,
but it's good to forage, it's good to learn,
it's good to fight, and finally earn our wage.

So here we are, you and me,
I see it's you and me.
A little darkness didn't hurt no one,
but my heart hates the lies that it has spun,
under the cover of night, without the light to see,
I see it's you and me,
It's you and me.

HEADLESS IN OHIO

Who let the midnight in
Into the path of the day
I'm feeling happier this morning,
and I ran the truth away
I read something about positive thinking,
I read something that's keeping me sane
Well, every fool is good for something,
and every something holds some blame.

Headless in Ohio, again and again and again

PICKING A CARCASS CLEAN

You asked me to change so many times,
but if I did, oh if I did,
I'm worried that I wouldn't be her
and you wouldn't be him.

So let the forces between keep rocking our boat,
and not cleaning the stars,
So the glare won't be gone and so all the fun,
from picking a carcass clean.

So let's agree for the very last time,
that perfection isn't dying alone,
let's keep the berth of sadness
inside its wiry home.

For you to be him and me to be her,
or for as long as we decide to reside.
Sometimes the stars need the brine of darkness
and nothing,
to let itself quietly reside.

QUIET HOLLOW

The loneliness of the day,
syncopated with the emergence of first light,
and ending with the dull hue of dark black.
You expect to feel lonely in the evening,
like the dormouse and the lone wolf,
you sleep and forget someone
knocking on your door,
and so you find comfort.

First light,
it is the morning dew and awakening,
your eyes nearly closed.
Your back hunched and your mind so slow that you feel
the quiet hollow.
Stuttering through to noon
and your loneliness is a smoking chimney.
Close your eyes for awhile
and sleep through this madness,
wait for the emergence of blackness,
and the hollow to quiet.
Seek solace in the universal coming together
of everyone feeling this way,
of the expected loneliness that is somehow dulled
by the magnitude of those arriving home.
Come evening it inspires your hand,
to lay with a loved one
or work to the late chimes of early darkened morning.
And you wonder whatever quieted your hand,
in the hushed light of day.

WHEN LOVED

When loved, love tends to forget
its alternate end,
of loneliness and empty hearts.
When childish youth sinks and your cup runs dry,
it fills with crimson and spills out from the heart,
it empties by morning and fills by night,
and handed around, quickly divided out.

When finally the right one comes
to embrace the haunted cup,
it slowly drains and fills its lonely heart,
stormy and unwise, wild and scorned.
Its memory has no glass to see its reflection,
it forgets its fire will burn and mark the skin,
so once filled and replenished
with someone's love,
love suffers a loss of memory,
and starts again.

NEW YEAR'S EVE

Another sunken afternoon,
beer breath, crisps packets
and re-runs of Looney Toons.
Bank accounts ripped apart
on drugs and Uber fleets,
I'm too old for all this pain, treachery and deceit.

Evening appears to broken,
forced sick, cold pizza and demons awoken.
Dark shutters, unquenched waters
spiraling out of control,
where the body hides your comfort
is where you find your soul.

New Year's Eve comes to town,
don't drink the water for the water doth drown.
Escalating feelings, shadows and morn,
up till the daybreak with your insides half drawn.
The Nairobi desert is up in my insides,
feelings repeated yearly
like the coming of the tides.

THE ONLY WAY IS HOPE

Just in time to throw myself
from the imaginary bridge
I see the light undertones of hope
before I know it,
I'm feeling clean
I walk around this world optimistic
seeing hope in reality TV

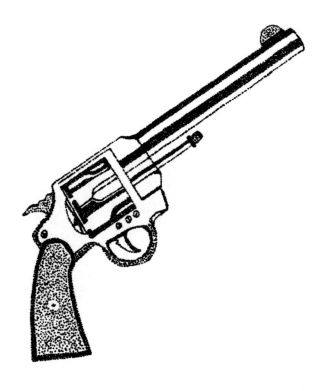

Kill Someone

KILL SOMEONE

There's a man out there talking, speaking in tongues
losing his hair, bleeding gums
Saying things about my sister, things about their son
If he don't stop soon, I'm gonna kill someone

He's got eyes of black and a hide of green,
Throwing out lines like a submachine,
Don't know why or what he really means,
Well he hasn't been there, and he hasn't really seen

He says he was a soldier, he told me that he served,
Well he never left the barracks, only a reserve,
Now he's taking it up with another racist word,
I think he lost the war, and he won the purge

Now he's fighting for justice and praying to God,
While he misspells his name and keeps his fingers crossed,
Everyone knows God's been dead since 1914,
He can't bridge the gap for the underneath

Take Him Down Some

He has four babies with four different girls
He has four houses, he has four worlds
But he has no money though he's wearing someone's pearls
And he'll take from your pockets
While he fumbles their curls

In his son, I can't see his father's eyes,
Because the boy is an angel, the boy doesn't lie,
Though he's still one of his lowly four,
His eyes may run but his blood won't pour

Take Him Down Some

He was bred from the devil, he was bred just to take,
Where they screw up their own in the belly of a lake,
Who the hell takes a baby to a dead man's wake,
When the dead man's a racist, the dead man's a snake

I'm gonna wake up in the morning and get myself a gun
Not to fire at anybody, just to keep him on the run
Just to drive in the screw, then rust it in the sun
Like he does to me, like he does to everyone.

Take Him Down Some

O' SWEET MARIE

O' Sweet Marie
I have waited oh so patiently
up here in this loving cloud
while you fumble for the crowd
O' Sweet Marie

I heard another sing your song today
while you glistened in my pain
and I fell to earth just like the rain
O' Sweet Marie

I don't know why I really care so much
am I so desperate to feel the love
after I have fallen so far from above
O' Sweet Marie

it may be time to let me go
and like my coming you should know
the sweetest things Oh Sweet Marie
are sometimes stolen by the crow.

O' Sweet Marie

I WILL NEVER

I will never
be that innocent white boy
the kind that stays close to home
and keeps with innocent company

I will never
be the guy working in an office
leaving at 8:30 every morning
returning with a paper for dinner at 6:00
with a white musky shirt

I will never
have a doctorate
and be able to read your pulse
or diagnose our children's coughs

I will never
go to church again
and be able to quote the psalms
or take communion
and know the saints to pray to

I will never
have the will to leave early
there is too much romance in the depths of night
but I will wake early with you

I will never
be able to buy you the house you deserve
or the endless summer holiday you need
I will enjoy every day with you
and learn to fix and nail

I will never
hunt animals
and neither will you
I put this in here to fill out the poem

I will never
learn to hold back
to not drink, to not shout, to not rave on
and be a quiet passive

but I will
be everything you need
and be everything else as well,
and I will never leave you
I promise

DEATH TO THE WOMB

How much does a cry for help cost,
when you don't have a NHS.
Well, too much for you and your friends I'm afraid,
said the voice in an ivory dress.
But what of those sickly and ailing,
crippled or unable to earn,
don't they deserve to be healthy,
should their needs be lit and then burned?

If they can't afford to work, or
if they can't afford to give,
then they shouldn't be expectant to receive
or for us to unscrew the lid.
They shouldn't be having children,
they shouldn't be out on the streets,
they measure their triumphs with laughter
and love not by their houses and fleets.
So that's why the cry for help costs,
that's why we refuse to give,
we see a happiness inside their souls,
their joy and an endless yearning to live.

We strive to earn and to collect,
to gather our things and to make,
we don't have time for comfort and joy,
we work till our feet doth ache.
So until they match our fatigue,
until they give and are screened,
their ailments will go on ailing
and justice will always be leaned.

For if they cannot find work or jobs,
then they must quickly go and move away,
leave all their family behind
and learn to pursue and prey.
For beasts will not suffer in silence,
for beasts will not curb to the tomb,
like beasts they must be treated and strive,
like beasts from the death to the womb.

My Favourite Hotel Diner

MY FAVOURITE HOTEL DINER

Flashing neon lights above the hotel diner,
scurrying winds outside and fleeting greetings
from one to another.
People watch the floor, scrunching their shoulders,
but then there is you.
The brightness, the lighthouse, the symbol of effigy.
Your sweet eyes above the wind
and your shoulders relaxed.
Everyone can't believe that you are here to see me,
inside the hotel diner with its neon flashing bright.

As I pull your seat, I see a tear roll down,
you drop your heavy bag and hunch over the bread and oil.
You cannot take this day, or the thought of one tomorrow,
and I have been a fool to think of you above the wind.

You poke and stab your food as you explain to me,
your parents, your job and this city,
are too much to stream underneath your bridge.
I tell you it will be okay, that I will move away with you,
as the neon lights flash and prod a silky purple hue.

She eats and gathers herself,
the tear removed and placed in her purse,
shoulders un-hunched,
and she rides away like Godiva again.
Everyone wondering why
she would eat with someone like me,
and what I must of said or done to make this lady cry,
in my favourite hotel diner,
my symbol of effigy with the neon burning bright.

I WONDER

I wonder oh I wonder
as I sit here and ponder
where do all the dying go
will we ever really know
I don't really mind or care
if I end up there
up in the clouds or out at sea
far to the north, unable to see
in Hades or in heaven
with the dial turned to eleven
floating on the River Styx
or buried under ancient burial bricks
make it soft and make it quick
while I'm shooting from the hip
make it easy, make it long,
with no more rights to make a wrong,
with no more bows left to tie,
with lightning shooting from my eyes,
lowered softly to the ground,
with not a murmur or a sound.

IRISH POEM

I wish I was cold
and blue to my bones,
and you would hold me
and then we would be so very warm

I wish I was sad,
with tears in my eyes,
and you would hold my hand and catch the rain as I cry.

I cannot see you, no matter how hard I try,
for I don't own the rivers,
and I'll never own the sky,
I'm not one for words, and I can't write it down,
but I'll be there
when you are lowered to the ground.

Sleeping with the Diamond

SLEEPING WITH THE DIAMOND

There are diamonds in the mine
the local people said
as they lifted up the coffin
and dusted soil from off his head
let's not be weary settlers and settle in this pain
this man has died for diamonds
this man won't die in vain

take the children from the schools
and let's ration all the food
with half a belly empty
they'll have something else to prove
send them back into the mines,
deep down into the depths
if the diamonds are too heavy to carry
stuff the pockets of the dead

the children come up coughing
crying for the need to sleep
for in the dark it's hard to see
as they dig into the deep
as their tools chime upon the rocks
with sounds to awake the devil
the diamonds glint all the minds
of the elders and their council

suddenly the call was made
they had come across the stones
and how the elders sang and dreamt
of having them in their homes
but all went quiet in the mine
and not another word was heard

as the cavern and walls
came crashing down
killing all the boys and girls
no teardrop hit the dusty floor
no cry plagued the sky
their diamonds pockets empty
their eyes remained all dry
the children's bodies were never found
and grief would never lighten
sleeping soundly in the mine
sleeping soundly with the diamond

TULUM

Serene and bright,
the crystal waters glow,
the depths untold and kept to our nightmares
while topless women glance to waiters.
The separation between nature and them
is kept by me in the middle,
seemingly holding both in place.
Fishing vessels run the shore,
seagulls follow from high,
the ancient ruin stakes its rights
to ownership and true power of these waters.

I can see my place in the middle,
between them and all of nature's rest.
I say a prayer to the ancient Gods
and thank them for having me,
for having the bronze nipples and sandals,
brought from Europe and America.
As the lizards stalk the sun
and lay down on account rocks,
I also say an ancient prayer for me.
Here in Tulum, where the ancient bricks may crumble,
yet its masters lay waiting,
watching us sleep.

THE TOWN GREEN

In this small town, unregistered and unnoticed,
where criminals not yet criminals commit offences.
Like rolling the disabled kid into a river,
stealing clothes off the washing line,
and kicking your head in over your football shirt.

Meaning consolation,
"These bullies will never leave," Mam says.
How am I supposed to find comfort in that
with a bloody head, I want justice now!
"You will laugh at them one day," she said.
So no wonder I moved away so early.
No wonder I have such a complex about home,
if I stayed, maybe I would have become them,
and rolled Jimmy into the river.

I don't see why we couldn't call the police.
But the police station is manned by one person,
and my Mam says,
"We shouldn't waste his time, or stop him from
getting criminals or drug dealers."
My eyes and face fell red. "THEY ARE DRUG
DEALERS, THEY ARE CRIMINALS,"
"Here!" Mam rolled her eyes,
"In this small town, pfft, criminals live in London."

I moved to London much to her delight when
I was seventeen. She was proud of me.
But the small towns, they harbour the real criminals,
shit throwers, bullies, animal cruelties
and rolling Jimmy into the river.
Unregistered and unnoticed forever.

ON TO THE NEXT

On to the next, on to the next,
don't stop, who's looking? who's paying?
On to the next.
New Romanticism is shit, Opera is elite,
Bill Childish said something like;
"Who wants to create something
that can't be copied,
who else will pick up and carry the next."
So on to the next.

Create like an amateur, love like an amateur,
make like an amateur.
Somewhere I became a Professional,
and I'm not sure where.
Barely a professional, but I'm omitted from the amateurs.
I'm forgetting where I got started,
and who I used to listen to,
who I used to look up to,
I long to be an amateur,
to create like an amateur.
On to the next, on to the next.

WEBMD AND GOOGLE

I woke up this morning breathing heavy,
my head filled with dread,
is it an ulcer in my stomach
or a tumour in my head?
I'm gonna check the internet
and see what's really going down,
WebMD and Google it,
and my thoughts begin to drown

Are you seeing double, yes, yes, I think I am,
is there a yellow to your pigment,
are your hands beginning to clam,
is your breathing heavy
and your lips riddled with drool,
are there lumps upon your back
and blood in your stool?

My heart is beating faster,
quick, quick, let's look it up,
am I too young for a heart attack,
should I pee into a cup?
do men have a uterus?
I have symptoms for that as well,
Stage 4 cancer of the eyeball,
and I've lost my sense of smell

I really shouldn't be driving
not with my housemaid's knee,
and the steering wheel is bending
as my heart beats irregularly,
I'm deep in my own psychosis,
the doctor needn't diagnose,

I'll be a freak upon the slab
surrounded by the white of student's robes

I enter in his practice with tears all in my eyes,
shaking like a leper looking to the skies,
he asks a simple question:
"So what is wrong with you?"
"I think I'm dying or close to death
I may even have bird flu.
My head is bloated, my lung collapsed,
this mole is red and sore,
my stomach lining has come undone
and has upturned medical law,
my eyes are frail, my sense of smell
has all but disappeared,
and I have a uterus, don't ask me how,
the symptoms I've fully checked and cleared,
this knee of mine is falling off,
and my toe it has gangrene,
I have a constant rumble and throbbing
coming from a hole in my spleen.
Just knock me out, kill me now,
and call your friends in white,
test me quick, I'm a medical marvel,
let them drool at the sight."

The Doctor he peered and shook his head,
"Please excuse me for being frugal,
but keep your stupid eyes away
from WebMD and Google.
Go back home and take a shower,"
he wafted with his big right hand,
"and leave this shit to me and stay away from things
you don't fucking understand."

JEALOUS OF ME

I know a man who is jealous of me, the only one I knew.
I used to look up to him when I was back in school.
But somehow, some way it all turned around,
and I don't know when it did, or when I was crowned.

I don't think he ever aimed too far or too high,
not that I did or do that would be a lie.
I followed in time with something he did,
while I let it out, he kept it well hid.
But somehow, some way it all turned around,
and I don't know when it did, or when I was crowned.

Things got in the way of me and of him,
my actions were mistaken and seemed full to his brim.
I did not notice that he was stalking behind,
and every word that I wrote was being underlined.
And somehow, some way it all turned around,
and I don't know when it did, or when I was crowned.

I have tried to remember a time when I was at fault,
but even if I did, I was a child, he an adult.
Why would he try to pass on something he did
and that he loved,
for then to grow cold and sneer from the echoes above.
But still I did not take or steal from his art,
though his enthusiasm and joy really helped at the start,
so somehow when I don't mention or credit his name,
he turns into a martyr and plays his jealous game.

So somehow, some way it all turned around,
and I don't know when it did, or when I was crowned.

POEM 99

when I was small I did not know it,
I just shook my head and clung to a leg,
then it left like a fleeting look,
without a memorable face,
to hook it

then I remember when I was older,
the barbarous sinking and uncomfortable dread,
but I found a way round it,
and did not even stumble,
I forgot what I had done

now I am here, wrapped in its cover,
drafts they are under my clothes and the blanket,
I snuggle up tight and close my eyes,
hugging myself and closing the door,
it has won and is winning,
it has struck and still striking,
and dread and the worry,
rocks me to sleep

Pie in the Sky

PIE IN THE SKY

It's anyone's guess, the root of this mess,
the ancient wall paintings
that are yet to fall down,
are kept here to remind us
that once we were less
are kept here to remind us
some things stick around.

Someone took the time,
to count between the stars,
those balls of gas that sit in the sky,
they are here to show us what lies beyond Mars,
that what teachers once told us was merely a lie.

DE-PRE-SS-ION

You're seeing things,
you're not seeing the in-between,
just the beginning and the end,
the seed and the frozen dead flower,
the engine and the rust,
who cares about the factory
and the car fallen to dust.

You're not tasting things,
you sit down at the table
and you quickly get up to leave,
the sterling china and the shining knife and fork,
putting on your coat and ringing that leaving bell,
who cares about dinner
when after tastes like hell.

You're not reading those good words,
you're lost between the cover and
the "other collections made by Penguin,"
the binding and the creased tracing paper,
the author and the publisher's mark,
who cares about that sweet book smell
when your head is in the dark.

You're not seeing the beauty of the misty mountains,
the endless roaming hills,
it's why we moved here,
these open spaces like time,
a simple life to appreciate the fallen leaf
and growing flower,
who cares about being reborn
when death is on your mind every hour.

I can feel the weight finally being pulled from my arms,
two giant birds from the mountain,
slashing at my shoulders,
marked but in the clear,
finally able to eat and see and reason without fear,
so raise a glass and drink your tears.

455

A smashed old phone,
chipped at the sides,
a loose office necktie pulled too tight,
people stop and people slow down,
what a time to feel alive,
there has been a crash on the 455.

All of these things laid on the ground,
nothing lays as still as the warbled groans,
a dust of sand sprinkled round,
oil and plastic, cracked yet silken,
mothers cover their children's eyes,
there has been a crash on the 455.

Flashing lights from miles away,
bright and syncopated, baited in breath,
it's too hard sometimes to see over the cars,
harder to let yourself turn away,
someone will receive a bad phone call today,
forever a day when safety lied,
there has been a crash on the 455.

For those who were called to bend and to save,
wrecked memories draw tight and the calendar marked,
the stories will be told on cold barren nights,
no names, no places but detail of breath,
though some will force forgetfulness
leaving as they drive,
there has been a crash on the 455.

For those who arrived too late at the back of the queue,
their hearts will both drop, lift and take account,
that they would ever have to
bear witness to this technological age,
of monsters at speed, scientists of gain,
while epiphanies from the giants of industry,
build these glutinous machines
will boast that few who choose to take a drive,
crash and burn on the 455.

The Rain in the Mountain

THE RAIN IN THE MOUNTAIN

Oh the rain keeps on coming
Oh the rain it keeps on coming
But from the gods upon the mountain,
they see no need to send us warning
Yet the flooding and its damage cripples the spirit
but not our longing
For we are hurt more by their betrayal than the rain coming
from the mountain

We praise the dimmer light and
the clouds blocking out the sun
We feel the winter darkness,
romance fills our ears and unites us everyone
the red leaves fall closer to our doors dragged by the wind
we see the beauty in nearly everything,
but hate the hurt it brings
For we are hurt more by their betrayal than the rain coming
from the mountain

We see them flash out lightning and
bellow thunder on us all
as though the light show speaks an apology
for all the trouble and strife they caused
but we love the setting as the clouds release
the tip of their godly guilt
we see the people once again raise their hands and praise
those on the hill

But we have not forgotten the pain it's caused,
we have not forgotten
what they have placed upon us,
we have not forgotten they did not warn us,

we have not forgotten that they have done this before,
    but we lift our hands tomorrow
       and bow our wetted heads.
    To the Gods on the Mountain.

LAY IT DOWN

Lay it all on the line
write it down
take it all away except the meat,
and the bones
don't forget to not think too much about it
record it,
record it all,
listen to it all,
finish it
delete everything with bravado
and without energy,
take those words,
take that recording,
give it to your friends

That's as close to being an artist
as you will ever get.

THE WAR

The infantry stand with their backs to battle,
pushed forward by those unknowingly
arming the enemies,
arming death with easy prey.
"Collect oh Collect you hooded beast,"
the Christians chant.
"Kill for us soldier, but do not come back,
we do not want to see you
unless you are dead," they cry.
The war takes place
and the Christians are honoured,
the poor boys and girls
who took on the path after failing in class,
now winning in death and dying.

Across the bloodied plain
the mirrored image tells the same sweet tale.
As the Nationalists sing heady anthems
and push forth the dead,
funny how the enemies look just like their foe.
Now I swear somewhere in someone's Bible
it says "Not Kill,"
I swear the old soldier comes home silently whispering
"War Is Hell,"
Or maybe that was something
Ernest Hemingway said.
The sons and daughters of congressmen
do not line the battlefield.
So we and others have to die there
happily instead.

INNER CITY

I moved out of New York City,
up the deep Hudson,
to live under a mountain.
To sweetly walk the green,
to sweetly listen to nothings,
to bury the need for fraught ties
and endless movements,
barring suffocating chimneys
and rid myself of boundless catacombs.

But time has come to go back to the City,
and to blacken the soles of my feet,
eat lavish food and have no money,
and live the beatnik dream.

I need to write something other than
how the mountain joins the river.
I need to write about other things than
abandoned train tracks
and nooks and forgotten crannies.
I need to let the smoke clasp to the rain above my head,
and let me really feel suffocated by my thoughts.
It's time for someone in uniform to shovel the snow,
and me to walk alleyways and heavy roads,
bone idle.

O to be lonely in a city,
a lonely inner city,
I'm moving back into the City to be with you.

YOU ME, YOU ME

I hate to think,
what would happen,
if you started to act like me.
Would I be able to walk the room
without your hand gracing my face.
Or a compliment casually dropped
when I'm at my weakest in the morning.
I would never have to turn off the lights
and you would kiss my head,
and I'd never feel empty or cold or lost.
I don't want me though, I really want you.
I want you to do those things,
without ever thinking.
Do these things without ever drinking.
But you can't or won't,
and that's the way it will be.
And I would hate to think what would happen
if I was to act like you.
You wouldn't worry, and I wouldn't be there.
The perfect separation,
You and me, you and me.

LET IT OUT, LET IT GO

Un-hear the un-heard
take back all of your voicing
un-see the coloured woe
and inhale what you did sing
for no one should seek perfection
as no one can stoop so low
rid yourself of godly notion
let it out and let it go

SHIRLEY AND IVER

He saw her singing how the river was bare,
her lips tresses notes like feathers and air,
he fell in love with her right then and there,
he promised to keep her afar, her afar.

He was a picker and she was a queen,
he had another and she had a dream,
maybe he was afraid of all the in-between,
but bounty was to keep them apart,
keep them apart.

Shirley and Iver alone on the road,
scared to be lovers, and what would unfold,
he couldn't know her and she wasn't told,
that they would never need part,
need to part, need to part, need to part.

He would watch her sing every day,
from the quiet of his table
by the quiet of the day,
etched into his memory to make her go away,
for he had another to keep,
another to keep.

As the hammer fell unsteady
under honey-dripped nights,
Tennessee was creaking and bleeding and bright,
she saw him weeping and dried up his eyes,
and wanted them never to part,
never to part.

Shirley and Iver alone on the road,
scared to be lovers, and what would unfold,
he couldn't know her and she wasn't told,
that they would never need to part,
need to part, need to part, need to part.

Awake with the memories of burning bright flares,
she remembered his longing
and he remembered her hair,
so many reasons to never leave there,
but time waits for no one and love,
love hits hard, love hits hard, love is blind,
love is unkind.

They drifted and parted on their separate ways,
went home to others, one carried his name,
but no one would carry what they wouldn't say,
That they would never need to part,
need to part, need to part, need to part.

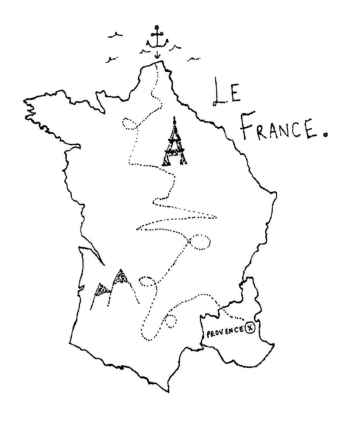

South of France

SOUTH OF FRANCE

Cramped hordes and
our Renault Laguna,
my sister's puke
smells like Ribena,
cigarette smoke,
half-eaten pizza,
We're in line for the ferry,
we're not going to Ibiza.

My mother's asleep
with her bobbing heads,
siblings on the back seat
with a greyhound on our legs
smile for the camera
driving up the ferry's ramp,
No jokes please, as we
get our passports stamped.

So much to do,
so much to see,
but Mam and Dad are desperate
for hospitality,
gin and tonics, beer and
my sister's on her phone,
I'm too busy scoffing my face
with giant Toblerone,
my Dad gets excited
as he leans back to relax,
We're finally on the ferry,
we're not paying any tax.

Head back to the cabin,
it's five to a room,
no porthole for this family,
it feels more like a tomb,
One sister has no pillow,
the others on the floor,
Four beds where five should be,
who could ask for more,
bunk beds have seat belts
to keep you safely in,
this is what you get
when you book it on a whim,
my Mam is drunk again,
she has her belt strung around her neck,
She's sleeping on the ferry,
she couldn't give a feck.

Awakened to the harsh sound
of the captain's morning horn,
Swiss chocolate aches and regrets
up at the crack of dawn,
one more stab at duty free
I'm running into debt,
the trip hasn't even started, and I have
the "Ghostbusters" video box set,
we go up to the deck,
we catch sight of sunny France,
as the gale beats our clothing,
my sisters do a rain dance,
I lean over the side and shout,
"we're never coming back,"
I spit against the wind,
which lands right on Dad's summer mac.

He chases me up and down the deck,
I barely make it out alive,
We're getting off the ferry
and have 500 miles to drive.

We're driving to the south of France,
we're driving night and day,
my Dad would run over Jesus Christ
if he got in the way,
our legs they ache
from cramp confines
and dare we shout or shriek,
our mother will scratch our legs to bits
'cos dad hasn't slept in weeks.

Our father dreams of rolling vines
of red wine and smelly cheese,
I wind down the window
if only to feel the summer breeze,
"Roll up that bastard window,"
as he bangs on his airbag,
I roll it and I'm promptly sick
into a Tesco plastic bag.

"Bloody hell,"
shout Mam and Dad,
as I wipe my mouth in vain,
200 miles to Provence,
the car smells like Ribena again.
Oh land of beauty, culture, food
and wondrous green trees,
We're not even halfway there, and
I'm sick going over the Pyrenees.

Tiny Citreons they swarm the right-sided road,
we're singing "Hallelujah,"
Everyone is covered in dog hair,
inside our Renault Laguna.
We pull over just for a quick second,
Mam is sat there on her knees,
scrubbing off my sick,
spraying lavender Febreze.
We set upon the road again,
not far, not far to go,
my sister's in the back seat
with the early stages of impetigo.
She keeps it quiet and
scratches softly,
not wanting to cause a fuss,
without us knowing she's as contagious
as nits on a school bus.
So ignorance is blissful,
living inside a tent,
we argued, talked, played and drank
and sang a sweet lament,
"Where did you get that rash from," Mam asked,
"from Sophie or back in school?"
"Now you must not play with other kids
or go back in the pool."

We laughed at her, my little sister,
miserable and all alone,
she longed for the holiday to end,
for us to return to home,
until my father intervened and
told her to feel happy to be alive,
until he noticed he had very same rash
creeping down his side.

"Bloody this" and "bloody that"
"curse you all to hell,"
"the holiday is ruined,
why does this ointment smell?"
Half the tent was theirs,
all disease and special cream,
like peasants during Medieval times,
plagued and locked in quarantine,
how could this be any worse
she screamed into our mother's ear,
failing to recognize
the early symptoms
of gastric diarrhea.

The long trip home
was fraught with songs
and stops at the pharmacy,
"MY DAUGHTER HAS A POORLY TUMMY,
thank you and *merci*."
But to no avail
they did not understand,
my Mam stuck to her guns,
she raised her voice
and pointed down,
"MY DAUGHTER HAS THE RUNS."
My little sister walked away,
too tired and ill to care,
to add to her woe
when showering,
she had squeezed aloe vera in her hair,
her hair like oil and grease now,
stuck to both sides of her head,
to make matters worse
her flatulence smelled similar to egg.

Not one to be beaten
not afraid to firmly stand her ground,
we all joined in and agreed with her
when she blamed it on the greyhound.

Now we are on our holidays,
some are sick and some are merry,
desperate to see the back of it,
and climb aboard the ferry.

ANOTHER ANGLE

If at first you do not succeed,
maybe you weren't supposed to win,
for if you fail for a second time,
your patience grows too thin.
You hate yourself, retire and flicker like a candle,
sometimes you gotta start from scratch
and try another angle.

IN THE DARKEST OF DARKS

Let the daybreak seek another victim,
one who has something else to see,
I'm wrapped up here in the darkest of nights,
and rooted like the tree.
Now I'm not preaching solace,
or feeling up or down,
it's just me raving for the night
and in the daylight I will drown.
How many more summers do I have left,
how many more in this youth,
so let the daybreak sleep under another stone,
and let me remain aloof.
For me and my brothers are roaming,
under the darkest of nights,
my sisters are singing and calling to us
for our hearing and our sights.
For one day I will not wonder anymore
and seek the realm of the dark,
I won't see romance in the stars,
and I'll prefer to light up and spark.
Today is not that day
and neither will tomorrow be,
when I am the rover no more, bright torch,
so go set some other soul free.

PLEASE BE UNDERSTANDING AND KIND

It's a mystery,
I have this dictionary,
and I can Google,
and needn't be frugal,
so why is writing today so difficult and hard,
the inside of my mind is burnt and charred,
but without fire,
of inspiration's singing choir,
it's strange with all my history,
that it must remain a mystery,
and not put it on the page,
especially in this new and accessible age,
or I could make things up and use my imagination,
far from my wheelhouse and station,
I'll watch a movie,
that will do me,
then I can write about something I have seen,
or a place I have never been,
but I'm really just putting it off,
I should be scraping the trough,
of my deepest tones,
telling my wildest unknowns,
to those who will listen,
let the satire drip and glisten,
let sarcasm and majesty reign,
play the sweet and proven game,
of writing at its most truthful,
when it seems both aged and youthful,
very real with a dash of fiction,
with perfect grammar and luscious diction,

let the reader be directed yet free
and told to roam,
where the dark and lucid wilderness
is never far from home,
today it's a mystery to me how to write like this,
I'm dangled over the dry and arid precipice,
of a writer, dried up,
with nothing coming to mind,
so if you are a reading this,
please be understanding and kind,
To my mind.

Sincerely,

ACKNOWLEDGEMENTS

The author wishes to thank the following:

Nicole D'Anna and her family

Stuart Ongley

Sharon Weisz

Mam, Dad and Paul

Natasha Janet and Rebecca Long

Granny Smith and Auntie Margaret

Teacher Mrs. Mills

Sven and his family

Jessica Gattone

Hilary Huckins-Weidner

And all my other family and friends

INDEX OF TITLES

Page

455	72
Ancient Cracks	3
Angela-Louise	22
Another Angle	91
A Parisian	14
Awoken Clean	16
Illustration: A Writer's Life	18
A Writer's Life	19
Blood Pumps Lilac	31
Illustration: Blue Cagoule	26
Blue Cagoule	27
Cafe Table Visions	4
Christmas Lights	11
Dark Road	7
Death To The Womb	52
De-Pre-SS-Ion	70
Illustration: First Memory	34
First Memory	35
Gotta Get Out	1
Headless In Ohio	40
Inner City	79
In The Darkest Of Days	92
Irish Poem	57
It's Good To Miss Someone	6
It's Good To See A Little Brightness	38
I Will Never	50
I Wonder	56

INDEX OF TITLES

Page

Jealous Of Me	66
Keeping Apart	24
Illustration: Kill Someone	46
Kill Someone	47
Lay It Down	77
Let It Out, Let It Go	81
Love Is Sweet	21
Martyr	37
Illustration: My Favourite Hotel Diner	54
My Favourite Hotel Diner	55
New Year's Eve	44
Illustration: Night Bird	8
Night Bird	9
On To The Next	63
O'Sister	12
O' Sweet Marie	49
Picking a Carcass Clean	41
Illustration: Pie in the Sky	68
Pie in the Sky	69
Please Be Understanding and Kind	93
Poem 99	67
Quiet Hollow	42
Real Love	28
Secular For Jesus	32
Shirley and Iver	82
Illustration: Sleeping with the Diamond	58
Sleeping with the Diamond	59

INDEX OF TITLES

                                                                                               Page

Title	Page
Illustration: South of France	84
South of France	85
Stare Down	25
That Sweet Refrain	10
The Only Way Is Hope	45
Illustration: The Rain in the Mountain	74
The Rain in the Mountain	75
The Shiny Penny	30
The Town Green	62
The War	78
Tulum	61
WebMD and Google	64
When Loved	43
You Me, You Me	80